Animal Neighbors

Fox

Michael Leach

PowerKiDS press.

New York

Published in 2009 by The Rosen Publishing Group Inc.
29 East 21st Street, New York, NY 10010

First Edition

Commissioning Editor: Victoria Brooker
Produced by Nutshell Media
Editor: Polly Goodman
Designer: Tim Mayer
Illustrator: Jackie Harland

Library of Congress Cataloging-in-Publication Data

Leach, Michael.
Fox / Michael Leach. — 1st ed.
p. cm. — (Animal neighbors)
Includes index.
ISBN 978-1-4358-4992-1 (library binding)
ISBN 978-1-4042-4569-3 (paperback)
ISBN 978-1-4042-4581-5 (6-pack)
1. Foxes—Juvenile literature. I. Title.
QL737.C22L42 2009
599.775—dc22
                                        2008005402

Picture acknowledgements
FLPA 8 (W. L. Miller), 9 (Roger Tidman), 12 (Martin H. Smith), 23 (David T. Grewcock), 28 top (W. L.
Miller), 28 right (Roger Tidman), 28 bottom left (Martin H. Smith), 28 top left (David T. Grewcock);
Michael Leach 15, 20, 25; NHPA Cover (Hellio & Van Ingen), Title page (Mike Lane), 6–7 (Daryl Balfour),
6 (top) Andy Rouse, 10 (Manfred Danegger), 13 (Mike Lane), 14 (Andy Rouse), 17 (Daniel Heuchlin),
18–19 (Suzanne Danegger), 22 (Manfred Danegger), 24 (Stephen Dalton), 21 (Andy Rouse); Oxford
Scientific Films 11, 21 (Mark Hamblin), 26 (Alan & Sandy Carey).

Manufactured in China

Contents

Meet the Fox

The fox is a bushy tailed member of the dog family. There are 12 species of true foxes, including the Arctic fox, the gray fox, and the red fox.

Foxes live throughout the world, except in Antarctica and Southeast Asia. They can be found in forests, farmland, and deserts, and in many cities and suburbs. This book looks at the red fox—the most widespread species in the world.

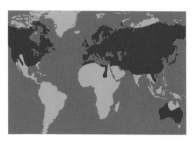

▲ The red shading on this map shows where red foxes live in the world today.

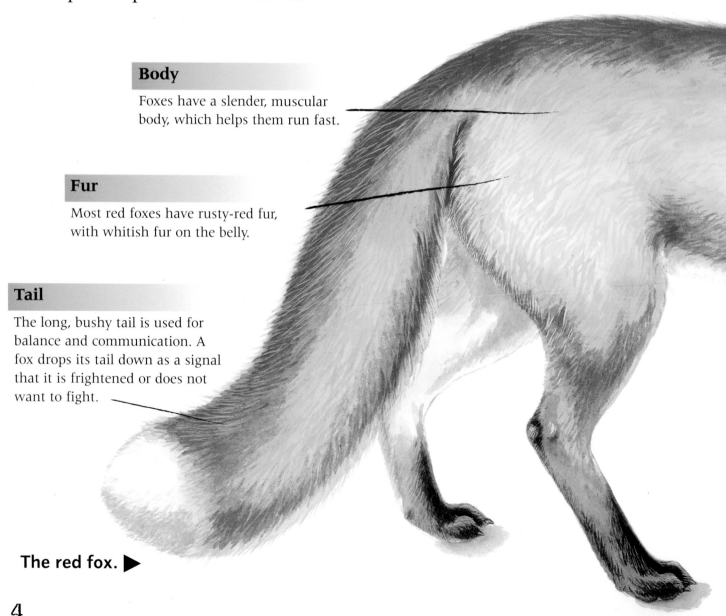

Body

Foxes have a slender, muscular body, which helps them run fast.

Fur

Most red foxes have rusty-red fur, with whitish fur on the belly.

Tail

The long, bushy tail is used for balance and communication. A fox drops its tail down as a signal that it is frightened or does not want to fight.

The red fox. ▶

4

Ears

Foxes have an excellent sense of hearing, which they use to track down their prey.

Eyes

The fox's eyes are large and forward-facing, which helps it spot its prey.

Teeth

Sharp, pointed canine teeth help rip into the flesh of prey.

◄ The red fox is larger than a domestic cat.

Legs

Long legs help the fox run fast when it chases its prey.

Claws

Unlike cats, the claws of foxes are nonretractable, which helps them grip the ground when they are running.

FOX FACTS

The red fox's scientific name is *Vulpes vulpes*, which comes from the Latin word *vulpinus*, meaning "cunning."

Male foxes are known as dogs, females are vixens, and young foxes are cubs.

Red foxes measure up to 27.5 in. (70 cm) long excluding the tail, and up to 16 in. (40 cm) tall at the shoulder. The tail can be 19 in. (49 cm) long.

Males weigh about 15 lb. (6.7 kg) and females weigh 12 lb. (5.4 kg).

The Dog Family

There are 35 species in the dog family. All dogs are predators—hunters that kill other animals for food. The largest member of the dog family is the gray wolf. This tall, powerful creature is strong enough to kill a fully grown deer.

Not all dogs hunt big animals. The tiny bat-eared fox in Africa lives mainly on insects and earthworms.

The gray wolf lives ▶
in Europe, North
America, and Asia.

Wild dogs are well adapted to living in different habitats. The Arctic fox has a thick coat of fur, which protects it from below-freezing temperatures of -40 °F (-40 °C).

The fennec fox has the opposite problem to the Arctic fox. It lives in the Sahara Desert. To avoid the hot sun, this fox comes out only at night. Its huge ears help to keep it cool by releasing body heat. They also give the fox excellent hearing, which helps it detect its prey.

▼ Bat-eared foxes are nocturnal hunters. Their huge ears pick up sounds of small animals moving around in the dark.

Birth and Growing Up

It is springtime, and a heavily pregnant vixen looks for a den, or "earth," to have her cubs. This could be a new tunnel that she digs, or an old hole made by badgers or other animals. In towns and cities, she might make an earth along a roadside, next to a railroad line, or even in someone's backyard.

At birth, the cubs are completely blind and deaf, born with their eyes and ears tightly closed. The one good sense they have is of smell. When they are about 10 days old, their eyes and ears slowly open.

▲ These newborn fox cubs huddle together to keep warm while their mother is out hunting.

Unless she is out hunting, the mother stays with her litter most of the time, allowing them to suckle several times a day. If the earth is disturbed by people, dogs, or other enemies, the vixen will carry the cubs to a safer place up to 2/3 mile (1 kilometer) away. When the cubs are 3 weeks old, the vixen starts to leave the earth for longer periods of time.

FOX CUBS

Newborn fox cubs are about 4 in. (10 cm) long and weigh about 4 oz. (110 g).

A vixen normally gives birth to a litter of between four and eight cubs, but as many as 12 have been recorded.

▼ Fox cubs carefully sniff the air for danger before moving out of the earth's entrance.

Early days

The cubs first leave the earth at around 30 days old. This is also when they begin to eat solid food. Their mother carries meat to the earth in her stomach. As soon as they see her, the cubs start to beg. As their mother coughs up the meat, the cubs gulp it as quickly as possible.

▼ A vixen feeds her hungry cub by passing food to it through her mouth. The partly digested food is easy for the cub to digest.

FOX CALLS

Foxes communicate with scent, sound, and body language. They can produce 28 different calls, each with its own meaning. A short, loud yap shows anger, a long yelp attracts a mate, and vixens use a soft whine to communicate with their cubs.

Cubs spend their early days close to the earth's entrance, quickly disappearing underground if danger threatens. On warm days, they laze about in the sun. They spend a lot of time play-fighting with each other, digging and playing games with sticks, bones, and anything else lying near the earth. These games strengthen the cubs' muscles and teach them the basic skills of hunting.

By the fall, the cubs are 8 months old and almost fully grown. One by one, the young foxes leave their mother and become independent. By the end of the year, they will all be gone.

▲ Fox cubs have such sharp teeth that they can injure each other when they are play-fighting.

Habitat

▲ These two foxes are about to fight over territory. Such fights are noisy and dramatic.

After leaving their mother, the young foxes must find their own territory. Each fox needs an area that provides plenty of food and shelter, and is not already home to any other fox. Every year, young foxes from many different litters compete for territories.

The strongest foxes win the best hunting grounds. The other youngsters may have to look for longer, but it won't be hard to find their own territory, because red foxes live in such a wide range of habitats. They can make their home in woodlands, farmland, towns, garbage heaps, and almost any other habitat. Once a fox has found a good territory, it stays there for life.

Each fox marks its territory with droppings and urine carefully left on stones and logs. This is called scent-marking. The scents are powerful smell signals that warn other foxes to keep away.

▼ A fox marks its territory with a spray of urine that will smell for up to two days.

TERRITORY

A fox's territory can be up to 7.7 square miles (20 square km).

Dogs usually have larger territories than vixens.

Fox territories sometimes slightly overlap, but neighboring foxes always try to avoid each other.

Town and country

The red fox's rusty coat is perfect camouflage in a woodland at night, keeping it well hidden as it stalks through leaves and undergrowth. But in other habitats, its coloring is less useful. Foxes that live in towns and cities can be easy to see against a background of asphalt and concrete.

▼ Foxes were originally animals of the forest. They have moved to other habitats, because many woodlands have been destroyed by humans.

Most urban foxes have never been in a forest or a field. Their behavior is suited to the urban habitat. Urban foxes stay hidden during the day, sleeping in abandoned buildings, underneath bushes, and even on roofs. They do not come out until dark, when most people have gone inside. Unlike urban foxes, rural foxes often hunt in the daylight, especially in winter, when food is hard to find.

COOL FOXES

Red foxes that live in northern Europe and Canada are specially adapted to their cool climate. Apart from having thicker fur than foxes living in warmer habitats, they are also not as tall. Long legs lose more heat than shorter legs, so their short legs help to keep them warm.

▼ Urban foxes find food in unusual places. A good sense of smell allowed this fox to find scraps of food on a bird table.

Food and Hunting

Foxes are omnivores. They eat worms, insects, voles, mice, rabbits, and a wide variety of other small animals, as well as plant food, such as grass and berries. Each adult fox eats just over 1 pound (about 500 grams) of food a day. They need more food in winter to keep warm.

▼ **Foxes are at the top of their food chain. Here is some of the food that foxes eat. (The illustrations are not to scale).**

Fox food chain

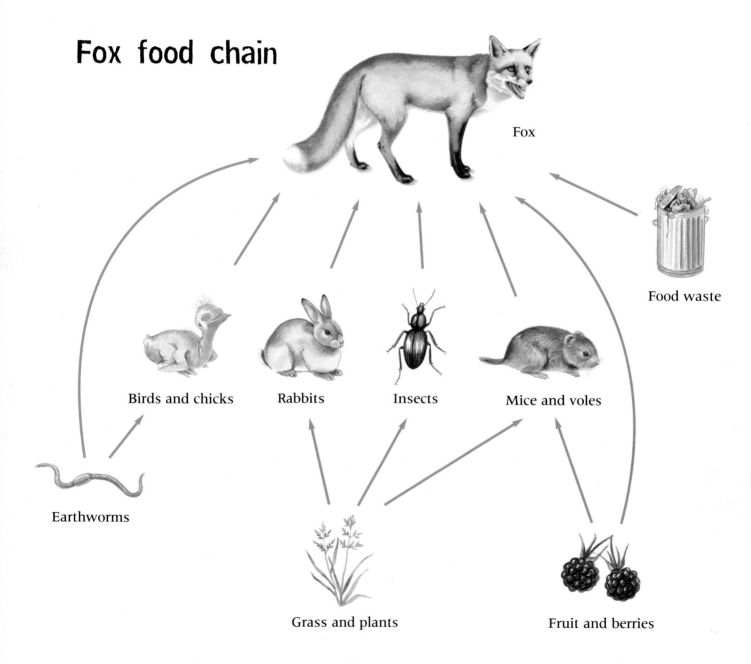

Fox

Food waste

Birds and chicks

Rabbits

Insects

Mice and voles

Earthworms

Grass and plants

Fruit and berries

The fox's diet changes throughout the year, according to the food available. In the spring, mice and voles are a source of food because it is their breeding season. As the young mice and voles leave their dens for the first time, they provide easy pickings for foxes.

In the fall, foxes eat fruit and berries. During bad winter weather, they eat the bodies of animals that have died in the cold.

Foxes also raid birds' nests on the ground and in low bushes, and eat the chicks or the eggs inside.

Some foxes raid farms ▶ **to hunt chickens, geese, or newborn lambs. If this becomes a habit, farmers can lose a lot of animals unless the fox is shot.**

Hunting

The fox hunts mostly at night. It is a quick and skillful hunter, using hearing, smell, and sight to find its prey. If its sensitive nose smells an underground nest of mice or voles, the fox will dig deep into the soil to reach it.

Foxes regularly search grassy meadows looking for mice, frequently stopping to look and listen. When they hear a rustle or see a slight movement in the undergrowth, they jump and pin the mouse to the ground with their front paws.

Foxes stalk bigger prey by silently creeping forward at first, trying to get as near as possible before being noticed. At the last minute, they sprint and pounce, immediately killing the animal with their sharp teeth. Sometimes foxes ambush mice and rabbits by lying near a burrow and waiting for them to appear.

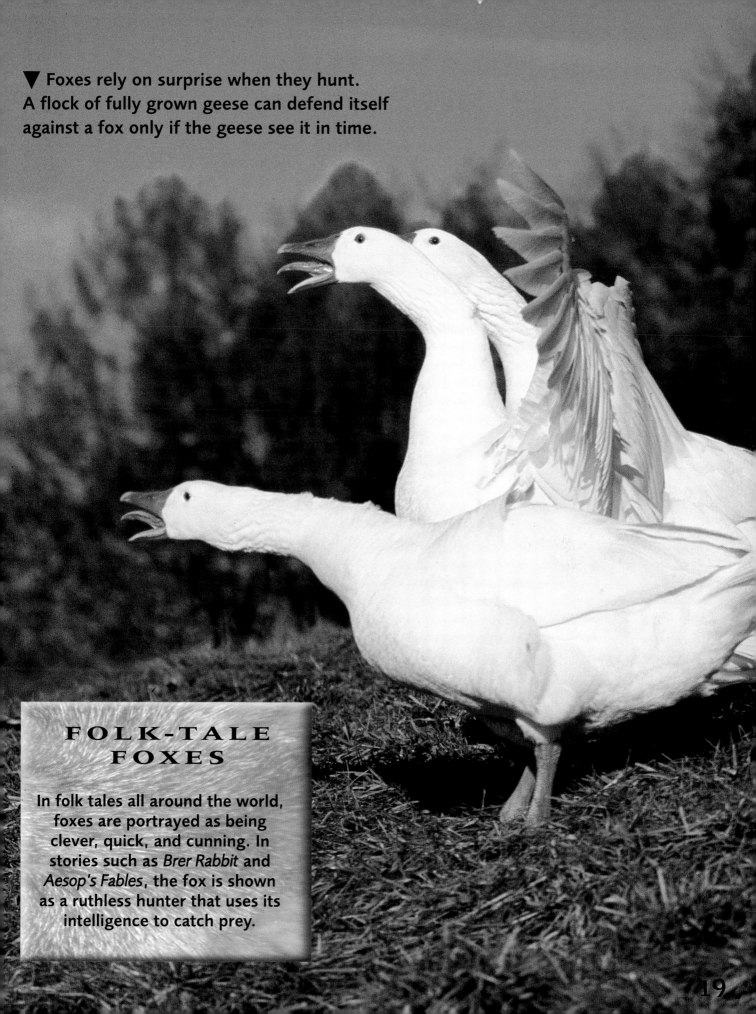

▼ Foxes rely on surprise when they hunt. A flock of fully grown geese can defend itself against a fox only if the geese see it in time.

FOLK-TALE FOXES

In folk tales all around the world, foxes are portrayed as being clever, quick, and cunning. In stories such as *Brer Rabbit* and *Aesop's Fables*, the fox is shown as a ruthless hunter that uses its intelligence to catch prey.

Storing food

Foxes usually eat their prey immediately, but after a big kill, they may hide leftover meat. They dig a shallow hole in the ground with their front paws, drop in the meat, and cover it with soil. They will come back to eat the food later. Storing food helps foxes survive days when there is little prey available, but other animals, such as badgers, often find and eat the food before the fox returns.

▼ Urban foxes soon learn which trash cans are likely to contain the best food.

FOX TRAVEL

The red fox was once found only in Europe. During the eighteenth and nineteenth centuries, when Europeans were settling in other continents, many foxes were captured and taken to the new settlements to help control the number of rats and mice there. Wild foxes now live and breed successfully in countries such as the United States, Canada, and Australia.

Food in towns

Urban foxes are useful to humans because they keep down the number of rats and mice that live in built-up areas. But apart from eating rats and mice, urban foxes have learned to take advantage of people's wasteful habits. They raid trash cans and garbage dumps looking for bones, crusts, and other food that we have thrown away. They visit trash cans outside fast-food shops looking for leftover fries and burgers.

Foxes are clever animals that know where to find easy meals. They steal dog and cat food from bowls and have even been seen entering kitchens to find food. All foxes will eat carrion, and they often search along roadsides, looking for the bodies of animals killed by traffic.

Foxes can be injured by tin ▶ cans and broken bottles when searching through trash.

Finding a Mate

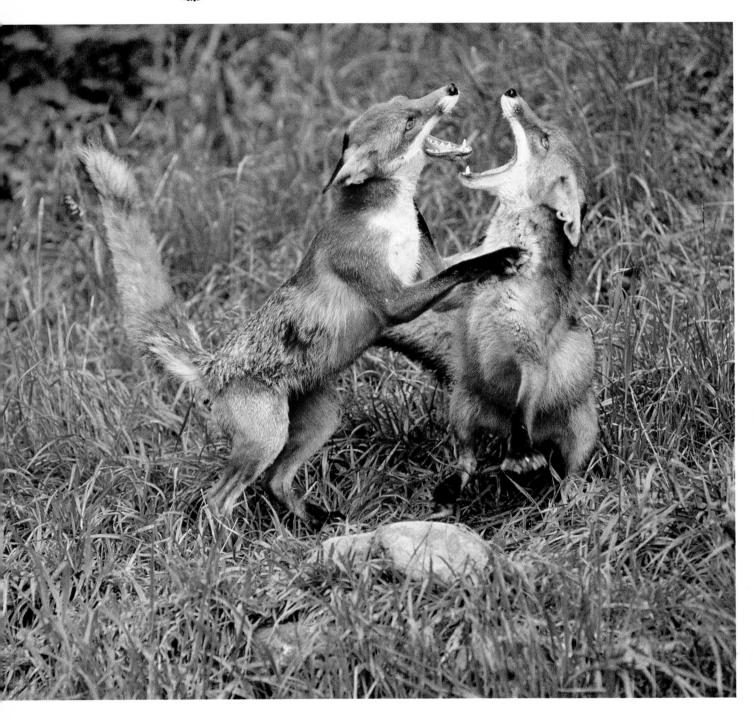

After they are a year old, foxes are ready to breed. The mating season is in January and February each year. There is a period of only three days when the vixen can become pregnant.

▲ Fights between male foxes may look dangerous, but the weaker fox usually runs off before it is injured.

As this time approaches, the vixen attracts nearby males with a long, loud call. The call can be heard over $^1/3$ mile ($^1/2$ km) away and several males usually respond.

When the males appear, they fight. The weaker males are driven away, leaving only the stronger, dominant fox to mate. He will stay with the vixen for a few days, before moving on to mate with one or two other females. About 55 days after mating, the new cubs are born.

▼ The vixen (below right) is often aggressive to the dog before she allows him to mate.

GHOSTLY CALL

Vixens looking for a mate give out loud, haunting squeals at night. In many countries, this sound was believed to be the cry of ghosts. Some people once thought it was a sign that a human was about to die.

Threats

Foxes can live to the age of 10 in the wild, but most die much younger. Urban foxes are sometimes killed by large dogs. Healthy adult foxes are too quick to be caught by most predators, but old, injured, or sick foxes cannot run fast enough to get away.

In some countries, large predators, such as bears, dig up and eat fox cubs from their earths. In Europe, most large predators, such as wolves and bears, have been wiped out by humans over the last 200 years, so people are now the fox's greatest enemy.

FOX MYTHS

The Incas of South America worshiped the fox as a god. But Europeans in the Middle Ages believed that foxes were associated with the devil. Many foxes were destroyed because they were thought to attract evil spirits.

◀ This large retriever has just killed a fox. In Europe, foxes have been hunted by trained hounds for centuries.

Road traffic is the red fox's biggest killer. In Britain alone, around 20,000 foxes die on the roads every year. Similar numbers are killed in many other countries. About 90 percent of foxes that live in towns are hit by cars at least once during their life. Even if they are not killed, they may be badly injured. Town foxes can often survive their injuries by eating scraps of leftover food while they recover. But foxes in the countryside usually die after being injured because they cannot run and hunt.

▼ Urban foxes like this one show no fear of cars, so many are hit as they cross roads.

Friend or foe?

Some people in the countryside do not like foxes because they prey on chickens, geese, and newborn lambs. Many farmers protect their livestock by killing foxes with traps, poisonous gas, shotguns, poisoned bait, and hounds. However, foxes also help farmers by eating mice and rats, which eat cereal crops and stored grains. In some areas where foxes were killed off, rodents increased so much that farmers had to bring in more foxes to help get rid of them.

▲ **Foxes that raid chicken sheds often kill more birds than they can eat.**

People in towns often welcome foxes and give them food. They can become so tame that they will take meat directly from a person's hand. In some towns, there are now more foxes per mile than in the surrounding countryside.

In many places, foxes are the main carriers of rabies. Millions of foxes have been killed in an attempt to stop this disease spreading, since it can affect humans as well as animals. Foxes can also suffer from other diseases such as distemper, which can wipe out large numbers very quickly.

▼ Pet cats and wild foxes treat each other with suspicion. Both could be hurt if they fight.

CAT KILLERS?

Some people in towns and cities believe that foxes kill and eat pet cats. But a healthy adult cat can easily defend itself against a fox. Cats and foxes are well matched and usually try to avoid each other.

Fox Life Cycle

1 The newborn fox cub is blind and weighs just 4 oz. (110 g). It is one of a litter of four to eight cubs.

2 Ten days after birth, the cub's eyes and ears open for the first time.

6 At the age of 12 months, the fox breeds for the first time.

3 At 1 month old, the cub leaves the earth for the first time and has its first taste of solid food.

5 Each young fox wanders alone until it finds a suitable territory.

4 The cubs leave their mother in the fall, at the age of around 6 months old.

Fox Clues

Look for the following clues to help you find signs of a fox:

Earth
A single hole in the ground, or a burrow beneath a shed or other building. Look for bones, feathers, or fur lying around the entrance.

Flattened undergrowth
In the spring, young cubs dig holes and play near their earth. The undergrowth is flattened and the ground disturbed. The cubs chew sticks, roots, and anything else near the earth entrance. These are covered with tiny, pointed tooth marks.

Droppings
Fox droppings are very black and often contain lots of hair or feathers. They are usually left in very visible places, such as on a stone, log, or high ground.

3–4 in. (8–10 cm)

Eyeshine
Fox eyes are highly reflective and glow a bluish-white color when they are caught in bright lights, such as car headlights. These can be seen up to 440 yd. (400 m) away. Often, only the eyes are visible, and the rest of the animal is totally hidden in the darkness.

Smell
Foxes have a powerful smell that is unlike any other European mammal. Their scent lingers for several hours after they have disappeared, particularly around the earth.

Footprints
Unlike cats, fox claws are nonretractable and can be clearly seen on the footprint. Fox prints are more oval-shaped than those of a dog.

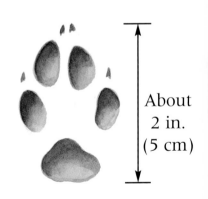

About 2 in. (5 cm)

Night calls
Loud, long calls at night are a good sign that foxes are nearby.

Hairs
Look for rusty-red hairs caught on twigs and fences.

Note: The illustrations are not to scale.

Glossary

ambush To attack by surprise.

camouflage The color or pattern of some animals that helps them blend in with their surroundings and makes them hard to see.

canine teeth Long, sharp teeth toward the front of the mouth, used for killing and tearing meat.

carrion The body of a dead animal that is found and eaten by another animal.

distemper A very infectious disease that usually affects dogs.

dog A male fox.

dominant The largest, strongest animal of the group.

earth The den of a fox.

habitat The area where an animal or plant naturally lives.

litter A group of young animals born at the same time from the same mother.

nocturnal An animal that is active at night and sleeps during the day.

nonretractable Claws that stay in one position, and cannot be drawn back like those of a cat.

omnivore An animal that eats all types of food, both animal and plants.

predator An animal that kills and eats other animals.

prey An animal that is killed and eaten by predators.

rabies A deadly disease that affects all mammals, including humans.

rodents Small animals, such as rats, mice, and voles, with sharp, gnawing teeth.

stalking Creeping silently and slowly, trying to catch prey without being seen.

suckle When a mother allows her young to drink milk from her teats.

territory An area that an animal or group of animals defend against others of the same species.

urban A habitat in a town or city.

vixen A female fox.

Finding Out More

Other books to read

Animal Babies: Mammals by Rod Theodorou (Heinemann, 1999)

Animal Classification by Polly Goodman (Hodder Wayland, 2004)

Animal Sanctuary by John Bryant (Open Gate Press, 1999)

Crafty Canines: Coyotes, Foxes and Wolves by Phyllis J Perry (Franklin Watts, 2000)

Life Cycle of a Dog by Angela Royston (Tandem Library, 2001)

Life Cycles: Cats and Other Mammals by Sally Morgan (Chrysalis, 2001)

Living with Urban Wildlife by John Bryant (Open Gate Press, 2002)

Natural World: Wolf by Michael Leach (Hodder Wayland, 2002)

Urban Foxes by Stephen Harris and Phil Baker (Whittet Books, 2001)

Welcome to the World of Foxes by Diane Swanson (Walrus Books, 1998)

What's the Difference?: Mammals by Stephen Savage (Raintree Steck-Vaughn, 2000)

Wild Canines of North America: Foxes by Jalma Barrett & Larry Allan (Blackbirch Press, 2000)

Worldlife Library: Foxes by David Macdonald (Voyageur Press, 2000)

Zoobooks: Wild Dogs by Timothy Levi Biel (Wildlife Education, 1997)

Web Sites

Due to the changing nature of Internet links, PowerKids Press has developed an online list of Web Sites related to the subject of this book. This site is updated regularly. Please use this link to access this list: www.powerkidslinks.com/ani/fox

Index

Page numbers in **bold** refer to a photograph or illustration.